D0605490

This is no longer
the property of
King County Library System

JAN 2015

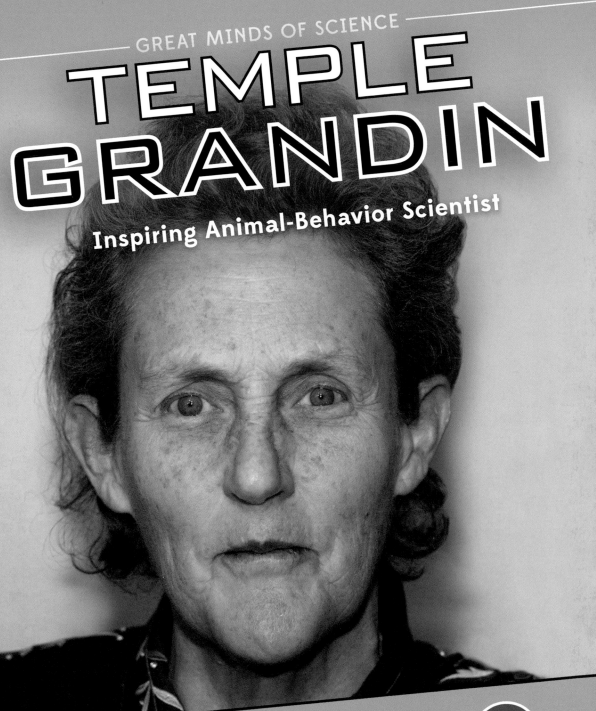

GREAT MINDS OF SCIENCE

TEMPLE GRANDIN

Inspiring Animal-Behavior Scientist

by Lois Sepahban

Content Consultant
Andy D. Herring, PhD
Associate Professor, Department of Animal Science
Texas A&M University

Core Library

An Imprint of Abdo Publishing
www.abdopublishing.com

www.abdopublishing.com

Published by Abdo Publishing, a division of ABDO, PO Box 398166, Minneapolis, Minnesota 55439. Copyright © 2015 by Abdo Consulting Group, Inc. International copyrights reserved in all countries. No part of this book may be reproduced in any form without written permission from the publisher. Core Library™ is a trademark and logo of Abdo Publishing.

Printed in the United States of America, North Mankato, Minnesota
042014
092014

THIS BOOK CONTAINS
RECYCLED MATERIALS

Cover Photo: Charles Sykes/AP Images
Interior Photos: Charles Sykes/AP Images, 1; Nancy Kaszerman/Zuma/Corbis, 4; Russ Einhorn/Splash News/Newscom, 9; Scott Bauer/US Department of Agriculture, 12; Tevonic, 14; Shutterstock Images, 17; R Carner/Shutterstock Images, 19, 43; John Epperson/The Denver Post/AP Images, 20; Temple Grandin, 24; PRNewsFoto/ Organic Valley/AP Images, 26; FeyginFoto/Shutterstock Images, 28; Pat Jarrett/ The News Leader/AP Images, 31; Koko-tewan/Shutterstock Images, 34, 45; Steve Jurvetson, 36; American Humane Association/AP Images, 39

Editor: Jenna Gleisner
Series Designer: Becky Daum

Library of Congress Control Number: 2014932491

Cataloging-in-Publication Data
Sepahban, Lois.
Temple Grandin: inspiring animal-behavior scientist / Lois Sepahban.
   p. cm. -- (Great minds of science)
Includes bibliographical references and index.
ISBN 978-1-62403-380-3
1. Grandin, Temple--Juvenile literature. 2. Animal scientists--United States-- Biography--Juvenile literature. 3. Animal specialists--United States--Biography-- Juvenile literature. 4. Women animal specialists--United States--Biography--Juvenile literature. 5. Autistic people--United States--Biography--Juvenile literature. I. Title.
636.092--dc23
[B]
                                                        2014932491

CONTENTS

CHAPTER ONE

GROWING UP WITH AUTISM

When Temple Grandin was in elementary school, she loved to create. She drew animals, made forts, sewed costumes, and built a sailboat. She had a talent for building with her hands. In other ways, though, Temple's childhood was a struggle. She was diagnosed with autism when she was three years old. This meant she had a difficult time communicating

Temple Grandin overcame struggles with autism to become one of the most influential voices in autism awareness and animal welfare.

with her family and friends. But in spite of these struggles, and maybe even because of them, Temple grew up to make the world a better place for others with autism and for animals.

Diagnosed with Autism

Temple Grandin was born on August 29, 1947, in Boston, Massachusetts. At that time, people did not know much about disabilities. But when Temple did not learn to speak, smile, or laugh when other babies did, her parents knew something was wrong. When Temple's younger sister and brother were born, Temple's differences became even more obvious. Her father thought that she should be put in a mental institution. But Temple's mother, Eustacia, wanted Temple to live at home with her family.

Eustacia found a doctor to help Temple. This doctor diagnosed Temple with autism when she was three years old. Eustacia was determined to help her daughter. She took Temple to a speech therapist who taught Temple how to talk. Eustacia hired a nanny who taught Temple good manners. And when it was time to start kindergarten, Temple's mother found the perfect classroom for her at a private school in the neighborhood.

Starting School

In her small kindergarten class, Temple's teacher and classmates treated her with kindness and respect. She was encouraged to create things. For the most part, elementary school was a happy time for Temple. But even with teachers and friends who cared about her, school was difficult for Temple. Like many people with autism, Temple has extra sensitive senses. The

Autism

People with autism often have a hard time understanding others. Others also often have a hard time understanding those with the disorder. People with autism do not always communicate in a way that nonautistic people expect them to because they sense things differently. Sometimes they repeat words or phrases over and over. They may also struggle to learn new things. At other times, they learn new things very quickly. In Temple's case, she had a hard time speaking her thoughts, but she was great at building with her hands.

loud ringing of the school bell caused her physical pain. Some scratchy fabrics bothered her so much that she could not think. And strong smells made her lose her concentration. With her senses overloaded, Temple had a hard time explaining to others what she was thinking.

Struggling to Communicate

What Temple did not learn until she was an adult was that she understood the world in a different way than her classmates. Temple thought in pictures. When she thought of a boat, for example, detailed pictures of all the different boats she had seen flashed through her mind. Temple had a hard time explaining her thoughts to others, making it difficult for her and her classmates to understand one another. Temple sometimes got so frustrated in her struggles to communicate that she had tantrums at school. Once she was even sent home for biting a teacher.

Middle school was an entirely different world for Temple. The local middle school was bigger. It had

Temple and her mother, Eustacia, right, pose together at the Emmy Awards in 2010.

more students. Most of them did not understand Temple's autism. Some of the students were mean to her. Temple still struggled to communicate. She often repeated the same words or phrases over and over. Some of her classmates called her names. When Temple got fed up with the teasing, she slapped the children who were teasing her. Eventually Temple was kicked out of the public school.

Boarding School

In the 1960s, Temple's parents sent her to a boarding school in New Hampshire called Hampshire Country

The Education for All Handicapped Children Act of 1975

In the 1950s, teachers in the United States were not trained to teach children with autism or other mental or physical disorders. As a result, disabled children often did not receive a good education at public schools. Many parents had to send their children off to special schools for disabled students. In 1975 a new law passed. It said that disabled children had the right to an education. It required public schools to give disabled children the help they needed so that they could go to school with nondisabled children.

School. At the boarding school, Temple was allowed to create and build projects. She made friends at the new school too. Best of all, Hampshire Country School had horses. Temple took on the responsibility of caring for them. She gave them food and water and cleaned the barn and equipment. Temple loved spending time with and caring for the horses.

But when it came to school, Temple still struggled. She did not like to study, and she began having panic attacks.

The panic attacks made her scared. They caused her heart to beat very fast. Her body would feel shaky and sweaty. These attacks sometimes lasted for hours. Even when she wasn't having a panic attack, Temple worried about when she would have another one.

The Squeeze Chute

Then during the summer after her junior year of high school, Temple's mother arranged for Temple to visit her aunt's ranch in Arizona. While there, Temple repaired fences, rode horses, and designed a gate that could be opened without getting out of the car. One day, as Temple and her aunt were driving on the property, Temple spied ranch workers putting cattle into an adjustable squeeze chute. Temple could not understand why the cattle were so calm in the squeeze chute. After the workers left, she asked her aunt to close her in a squeeze chute so she could see how it felt. Being locked in the squeeze chute had a magical effect. Temple's anxiety went away. She felt

Two men inspect a cow for ticks, while the cow is kept still and calm in a squeeze chute.

calm and peaceful. And that good feeling lasted even after she got out of the squeeze chute.

Over the summer, Temple had discovered she shared the same nervous feelings as cattle. She also found out that the cattle squeeze chute could help calm those feelings. When it was time to return to school, Temple brought these new ideas with her.

Temple Grandin did not always fit in. Other children sometimes bullied her and called her names. In the passage below, Temple describes her experiences with bullying and how she learned to cope with bullies:

> *Teasing hurts. The kids would tease me, so I'd get mad and smack 'em. That simple. They always started it; they liked to see me react. . . . My new school solved that problem. The school had a stable and horses for the kids to ride, and the teachers took away horseback riding privileges if I smacked somebody. After I lost privileges enough times, I learned just to cry when somebody did something bad to me. I'd cry, and that would take away the aggression. I still cry when people are mean to me. . . . Nothing ever happened to the kids who were teasing.*
>
> *Source: Temple Grandin and Catherine Johnson.* Animals in Translation: Using the Mysteries of Autism to Decode Animal Behavior. *New York: Scribner, 2005. Print. 2.*

What's the Big Idea?

Temple Grandin could not make others stop bullying her. She could only change how she reacted. Take a close look at this passage. What is she trying to say about her experiences with bullies? Pick out two details she uses to make her point.

CHAPTER TWO

BECOMING A SCIENTIST

Back at the Hampshire Country School, Temple decided that she wanted her own squeeze chute. She collected leftover pieces of wood from around the school and built one similar to the one at the ranch in Arizona. Some people at the school thought Temple's squeeze chute was strange and that it might even harm her. They did not want her to use it. But Temple's science teacher,

After graduation from Hampshire Country School, Temple attended Franklin Pierce College, which was in the same small town of Rindge, New Hampshire.

Mr. Carlock, had an idea. He said if Temple could use science to prove that her squeeze chute really worked on people, she could keep it.

Squeeze Chute Experiment

Temple went to work designing a science experiment. The experiment became her fixation. Some of her classmates volunteered to get into the squeeze chute. While they were in it, Temple asked them how they felt. Many of them said they felt calm too. The experiment helped Temple prove the chute worked.

Toward the end of high school, Temple knew she would have to become a better student if she was going to get

Fixations

Fixations are common in people with autism. Those who have the disorder sometimes develop a fixation on an object or idea. They put all their energy and focus into that one object or idea. Temple's squeeze chute experiments became her fixation. She wanted to understand how and why the squeeze chute worked for people and cattle. She read scientific articles to learn even more about cattle.

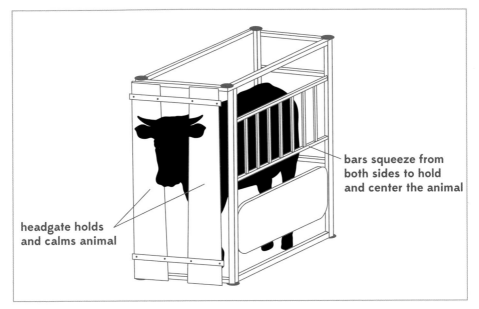

bars squeeze from both sides to hold and center the animal

headgate holds and calms animal

Cattle Squeeze Chute

This image shows a cattle squeeze chute. A squeeze chute holds a cow safely in place for examinations or veterinary treatment. After reading about Temple Grandin's experiments with a squeeze chute, what did you imagine one looked like? How has that idea changed? How does seeing this squeeze chute help you better understand Temple's experiments?

into college. She studied and worked harder in her classes. By the time she graduated from high school in 1966, Temple was already on the road to becoming a scientist.

Studying Cattle in College

After high school, Grandin attended Franklin Pierce College in Rindge, New Hampshire. She

Reading Animals

Grandin says she feels a lot of fear, much like a prey animal. This helps her to understand animals in a way that most people cannot. Fear is important for prey animals because it helps keep them alive. Prey animals must always be ready to run, swim, or fly so that they don't become a predator's lunch. For this reason, prey animals are more aware of tiny details in their environment. Any changes to those tiny details can cause them to become frightened. Because Grandin also sees those tiny details, she is able to read frightened animals' behavior. She helps people who care for animals understand the animals better.

continued her squeeze chute experiments. She graduated in 1970 and then went to Arizona State University to study animal science. She wanted to observe cattle in different kinds of cattle chutes. She visited approximately 50 feedlots in Arizona and Texas. Every feedlot she visited created a different picture in her brain.

In the 1970s, animal scientists did not focus on what animals thought and felt or how their feedlots were designed. They focused on keeping

In college Temple observed cattle in feedlots to learn more about the animals' behavior.

livestock healthy. But Grandin noticed things about cattle that others did not. By comparing all the different feedlots she visited, Grandin saw that some designs worked better for the animals than others.

She knew that she could design better systems and that her systems would improve the lives of cattle.

CHAPTER THREE

DESIGNING BETTER FACILITIES

While she was at Arizona State University, Grandin began to make a name for herself. She already knew that her feelings and experiences allowed her to relate to cattle in a special way. She understood the cattle's pain when they were hurt by badly designed chutes. And she could see the little things that frightened the cattle—little things that other people missed, such as

While most people would find this situation dangerous, Grandin finds peace while surrounded by cattle.

a jacket hanging on a fence or a shadow that looked like a hole. Grandin became good at interpreting how these little things affected the cattle. She knew that taking away the jacket or changing the lighting to get rid of the shadow would calm the cattle's fear.

Do Animals Have Emotions?

Grandin's designs consider animals' welfare and comfort. When she began her work with facilities that handled livestock, many people told her that the animals did not suffer because they did not have the same feelings as people. But Grandin disagreed. She thought that, like us, animals experienced fear and happiness. So she made it her goal to design facilities that minimized negative emotions, such as fear, and promoted positive emotions, such as calmness.

Designing Better Dip Vats

In 1972 Grandin wrote magazine articles about her observations of and work with cattle. She also wrote about feedlot and squeeze chute design. So in 1978, when John Wayne's Red River Feedyard in Arizona needed a better design for a dip vat, the company asked Grandin to help.

A dip vat is a pool of medicated water that cattle must walk into. The medicated water kills the bugs on their skin. If the bugs are not killed, they can make the cattle sick.

Grandin got to work designing a dip vat that made cattle comfortable. Her goal was to get cattle to walk into the dip vat and out the other side calmly. She knew a concrete ramp with bumps and grooves would be less frightening than a slippery metal ramp. Her ramp design also included a shallow slope to the water. Cows did not want to walk down steep ramps. On the shallow slope, however, the cattle calmly walked into the water.

Ranchers and livestock facility managers were impressed with Grandin's designs. When Corral Industries in Arizona needed new chutes built, they asked Grandin to help them with the design. Grandin understood two things about cattle that made her designs different and better. First, she knew that cattle wanted to go back to where they had started.

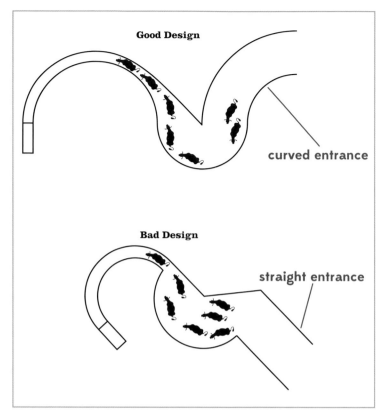

Cattle Chute Designs

The diagrams above are examples of a good cattle chute design and a bad cattle chute design. How are they similar? How are they different? Using what you have learned in this chapter about how animals think visually, what do you think makes one cattle chute better for cattle than the other?

And second, she knew that cattle moved in a circular way to get there.

Unique Designs

Grandin noticed that straight chutes allowed cattle to see the workers at the facility. Often, the cattle could see what was happening at the end of the chute and became afraid. They would try to get away from the workers. To avoid this, Grandin's designs had curved chutes or walkways. This way the cattle couldn't see the workers and didn't know what was happening ahead.

Grandin also noticed that cattle slipped and fell at many facilities. When that happened, the cattle could break their legs and be unable to walk. A fallen cow might cry out in pain. Hearing their herdmate's cry caused other cattle to cry out in fear. So Grandin's designs had floors with nonslip surfaces.

Packing Plant Chutes

A packing plant is a facility where livestock are taken to be slaughtered, or killed to make meat products. When animals arrive at a packing plant, they are unloaded from trucks and taken to a crowding pen, which holds many—often 30 to 40—animals at once. From the crowding pen, animals go through a single-file walkway, or chute, to the place where they are killed. Grandin's research and designs have helped make packing plants less scary for livestock.

Grandin speaks with George Siemon, left, chief executive officer of Organic Valley and supporter of the humane treatment of animals, in 2010.

Grandin's designs made ranchers happy and improved the lives of cattle. Her designs considered the cattle's comfort and well-being. And that meant fewer injuries and healthier cattle. More important, though, Grandin cared about cattle at packing plants and feedlots. She wanted their lives to be as pain-free as possible. She believed that even cattle that were going to be killed for their meat deserved a good life.

EXPLORE ONLINE

Chapter Three discusses some of the ways autism has helped Grandin design and create better facilities for livestock. The website below also focuses on autism. As you know, every source is different. How is the information given on the website different from the information in this chapter? What information is the same? How do the two sources present information differently? What can you learn from this website?

Autism
www.mycorelibrary.com/temple-grandin

CHAPTER FOUR

CREATING BETTER LIVES FOR ANIMALS

Grandin earned her doctoral degree in 1989. By this time, she had realized that other people did not see the world the same way she did. Based on her work with cows and horses, Grandin thought that the way she thought in pictures might be similar to the way cattle thought. She knew that she had to teach others to think more visually. Because once people could think more

Grandin graduated and earned her doctoral degree from the University of Illinois in 1989.

visually, they would have a better understanding of what cattle experienced. And once people had a better understanding of what cattle experienced, they would care more about making cattle's lives better.

Teaching Animal Science

Grandin was thankful for the mentors in her life, such as Mr. Carlock, who helped her become a scientist. She wanted to become a mentor and teacher herself. After earning her doctoral degree, she became an animal science professor at Colorado State University in Fort Collins, Colorado. There, she began teaching students about animal welfare and how to understand the way animals think.

Animal Audits

But students were not the only ones interested in learning more about Grandin's ideas about caring for animals. In the 1990s, many people became more interested in the treatment of animals. Animal welfare groups wanted companies, such as the fast-food

Grandin has given speeches across the country, helping others understand animal behavior.

restaurant McDonald's, to make sure livestock facilities treated animals with care. McDonald's bought more beef than any other company in the United States in the 1990s. So when McDonald's finally decided to purchase meat only from facilities that treated animals with care, US packing plants had to change their ways. But McDonald's needed an audit system, or a way of checking, to make sure workers at these facilities were treating animals with care. McDonald's turned to Grandin. Grandin created a system that observed and measured animal handling at the meat plants. Using her system, auditors observed the way animals were treated. If facilities did not pass certain tests, McDonald's and other companies chose not to buy the facility's meat products. Packing plants wanted to continue working with McDonald's, so they agreed to treat cattle with more care.

Grandin's Audit System

Grandin's audit system focused on cattle behavior. The auditor counted the number of cattle that limped, fell down, mooed in fear, and were shocked with an electric cattle prod. If too many cattle fell down, mooed, or limped, the facility failed the test. And McDonald's would not buy their beef.

New Rules for Chickens

In 1997 McDonald's asked Grandin to design

an audit system for chicken facilities. Grandin visited chicken packing plants and egg-laying facilities. At the packing plants, she saw workers drive over live chickens. She saw them break chickens' wings when they picked the birds up. Grandin made new rules. Sick chickens had to be killed in ways that would not cause suffering. Auditors counted the number of chickens with broken wings. If more than 1 percent of the chickens had broken wings, the facility failed.

When Grandin visited egg-laying facilities, she saw more signs of abuse.

Caring for Other Livestock

Grandin also works to improve the lives of other livestock, including pigs. After visiting pig farms, she noticed the stalls for pregnant female pigs, or sows, were so small that sows could not even turn around in them. Many pig farms in the United States still use small stalls. But Grandin continues to promote improved ways of caring for pregnant sows, such as placing them in larger stalls. She hopes that one day people will force pig farms to make changes the way cattle operations have.

Grandin encourages egg-laying facilities to use larger cages that allow hens to lie down next to instead of on top of one another.

Hens lived their whole lives in cages the size of half a sheet of letter-sized paper. They were so crowded into cages that they slept on top of one another. Most laying hens in the United States still live in cages too small for them to turn around in. Grandin promotes chicken welfare, hoping that one day hens' lives will improve. In addition to adopting her chicken-handling audit system, Grandin encourages facilities to use cages that have wider door openings so that chickens are not injured when they are taken out.

In some ways, Grandin's success in designing and changing livestock facilities is because of her experience with autism. The unique way she views the world through her senses is similar to how animals view the world. Her feelings of fear and anxiety help her understand animals' feelings of fear. By combining her love for animals with the special abilities she has as an autistic person, Grandin has helped make the lives of livestock better.

FURTHER EVIDENCE

Chapter Four describes how farm animals are often treated in the United States. What is the main point of this chapter? What evidence can you find in the chapter to support the main point? Learn more about livestock at the website below. Find a quote from the website that supports this chapter's main point. Write two or three sentences explaining how the quote relates to the information in this chapter.

Lives of Livestock

www.mycorelibrary.com/temple-grandin

CHAPTER FIVE

HELPING OTHERS WITH AUTISM

Because Grandin's experience with autism is so well known, she allows doctors and scientists to study her in order to help others with autism. In 1987 doctors took a scan of Grandin's brain. They compared the picture of her brain to other brain pictures, both from autistic and nonautistic people. The pictures helped them understand the ways an autistic brain is different.

In 2010 Grandin spoke at a conference about the importance of autistic thinkers, such as herself, who think in pictures.

Grandin's Books

Grandin has written multiple books, including two autobiographies. Her first autobiography, *Emergence: Labeled Autistic* (1986), tells the story of her personal experience with autism. Her autobiographies introduce autism to the world to help people better understand it. Since then she has written or helped write more than ten books about animals and autism. Some of her most popular books include *Thinking in Pictures* (1995), *Animals in Translation: Using the Mysteries of Autism to Decode Animal Behavior* (2005), *Animals Make Us Human: Creating the Best Life for Animals* (2009), and *Making Animals Happy* (2009).

Allowing others to learn about autism through her personal experience is one way that Grandin makes the world a better place for all people.

Today, Grandin speaks to groups all over the world. Her goal is to teach people about autism and animals. Simply by telling her story, Grandin has helped people with autism. Being a famous face of autism has given Grandin an opportunity to share what helped her overcome the challenges of autism. Her own experiences with

AMERICAN HUMANE ASSOCIATION
and
THE FORT WORTH LEADERSHIP COMMITTEE,
MR. ED SHIPMAN, CHAIRMAN
Welcome you to
THE
NATIONAL HUMANITA
AWARD
DINNER

Grandin was awarded the National Humanitarian Medal in 2011 for her work in improving animal welfare and the livestock industry.

extra sensitive senses has given parents and doctors ideas for helping children with autism. The squeeze chute Grandin built in high school is one example. Many autistic people find that feeling firm pressure, as in Grandin's squeeze chute, calms their anxiety.

Grandin's Impact on the World

Today, half of the cattle in the United States and Canada are handled in meat plants that use Grandin's designs. And around the world, companies use her audit system to monitor livestock handling.

Temple Grandin was diagnosed with autism when she was only three years old. But she used the gifts of autism, including thinking in pictures and experiencing the world through her senses, to improve the lives of animals and others with autism. And in improving the lives of animals and other autistic people, she has made her own life better.

Temple Grandin the Movie

In 2010 cable channel HBO premiered *Temple Grandin*, a movie about Temple Grandin and her impact on animal welfare and autism awareness. Actress Clare Danes starred as Grandin. The movie won a Golden Globe Award and many Emmy Awards. Grandin has said that she loved the movie and how it shows her experience and experiments.

Grandin encourages parents and schools to focus on hands-on learning. She worries that few young people will pursue careers in fieldwork, observing and studying animals, because they spend too little time outside:

> Today many children have little time for unstructured play outdoors where they can explore and get interested in the natural world. Childhood interests in animals or plants are often the reason a person goes into a career that involves fieldwork. Unstructured outdoor play also teaches valuable problem-solving skills. . . . I see all kinds of problems with college students who have never had an art class or built anything themselves. This lack of hands-on experience really hurts their understanding of how different things relate to each other in the real world.

Source: Temple Grandin and Catherine Johnson. Animals Make Us Human: Creating the Best Life for Animals. Boston: Houghton Mifflin, 2009. Print. 252.

Consider Your Audience

Review this passage closely. Grandin wrote this for an adult audience. Rewrite this passage for your friends. Write a blog post conveying this same information for the new audience. How does your new approach differ from the original text and why?

Animal Welfare

Because of Temple Grandin, people are aware that animals think and feel. Grandin has helped make sure that large fast-food companies buy meat only from farms that treat animals with care. Grandin gives speeches around the world to teach people how to make life as good as possible for animals.

Autism Awareness

Because of Temple Grandin, people with autism are treated with greater respect. Autistic people think differently than nonautistic people. Grandin has shown that these differences can improve the world. Grandin's different way of thinking has improved the world for animals and autistic people. Grandin's example shows that autistic people are capable of many achievements.

Packing Plants

Because of Temple Grandin, 50 percent of the packing plants in the United States have been designed in such a way that animals do not suffer before they are killed. The cattle and pigs at these packing plants are calm instead of frightened.

STOP AND THINK

Say What?

Reading about Temple Grandin's impact on autism awareness and the handling of livestock can mean learning a lot of new vocabulary. Find five words in this book that you have never seen or heard before. Use a dictionary to find out what they mean. Then write the meanings in your own words. Use each word in a new sentence.

Surprise Me

Chapter Four discusses Temple Grandin's impact on the treatment of farm animals. The way livestock are treated can be interesting and surprising. After reading this book, what two or three facts about the way livestock are treated did you find the most surprising? Write a few sentences about each fact. Why did you find them surprising?

Take a Stand

This book discusses what happens to animals at packing plants. Do you think it matters how animals are treated at packing plants? Write a short essay explaining your opinion. Make sure to give reasons for your opinion, as well as facts and details that support those reasons.

Tell the Tale

Chapter One of this book discusses Temple Grandin's experience with the cattle squeeze chute. Write 200 words that tell the story of Grandin's first time inside the squeeze chute. Be sure to set the scene, develop a sequence of events, and write a conclusion.

GLOSSARY

animal science
the study of farm animals, or livestock, that are owned and controlled by humans

audit
a careful check or review

boarding school
a school where students live during the school year

chute
a narrow passage through which things travel

diagnose
to identify a disease by observing its signs and symptoms

feedlot
an open-air facility that houses and feeds cattle

fixation
an obsessive interest in something

observe
to watch something closely in order to learn something about it

packing plant
a facility that converts farm animals into meat and various by-products for human use

squeeze chute
an adjustable stall built to hold cattle while they are examined

welfare
a person or animal's health, comfort, and happiness

LEARN MORE

Books

Grandin, Temple, and Catherine Johnson. *Animals in Translation*. New York: Scribner, 2005.

Grandin, Temple, and Catherine Johnson. *Animals Make Us Human*. Boston: Houghton Mifflin, 2009.

Montgomery, Sy. *Temple Grandin: How the Girl Who Loved Cows Embraced Autism and Changed the World*. Boston: Houghton Mifflin, 2012.

Websites

To learn more about Great Minds of Science, visit **booklinks.abdopublishing.com**. These links are routinely monitored and updated to provide the most current information available.

Visit **www.mycorelibrary.com** for free additional tools for teachers and students.

INDEX

ABOUT THE AUTHOR

Lois Sepahban has taught every grade from kindergarten to high school. She lives on a farm with dogs, cats, goats, and chickens. In her free time, she reads books, writes stories, and rescues animals.